Now boy, let me give you a piece of advice," advises the bushwhacker in Robert Benton's *Bad Company*. "If you're gonna pull a gun on somebody, which happens from time to time in these parts, you better fire about a half a second after you pull it, because most men aren't as patient as I am."

PRECEDING PAGE: John Wayne in *The Horse Soldiers*, 1959. RIGHT: cowboy extras. Who hasn't longed to be buried with a five-day stubble and his boots on?

Thunder IN THE Dust

Classic Images of Western Movies

John R. Hamilton

Text by John Calvin Batchelor

Stewart, Tabori & Chang
New York

Published by Stewart, Tabori & Chang, Inc.
740 Broadway, New York, New York 10003

The author acknowledges his debt to Phil Hardy's *The Western*
(William Morrow & Co., 1983) and to Michael Alexander's
translation of *Beowulf* (Penguin Books, 1977). The dialogues from
the western movies are transcriptions made by the author while
viewing them on video cassette recorder, and any errors are
regrettable and the author's.

Library of Congress Cataloging-in-Publication Data

Hamilton, John R. (John Ralph), 1923–
    Thunder in the dust.

    1.   Western films—History and criticism.   I.   Title.
PN1995.9.W4H35   1987   791.43'09'093278   87-10767
ISBN 1-55670-006-7

Distributed by Workman Publishing
1 West 39 Street, New York, New York 10018

Printed in Japan

10 9 8 7 6 5 4 3 2 1

PAGE 8: the legendary cowboy shoot-out in *Silverado*
pits good against evil. PAGE 9: director John Ford.

For my children, Elizabeth, Michael, Brian, and
John, Jr., and for the encouragement and help of
my wife, Regina—thank you all.

—JOHN R. HAMILTON

Thunder in the Dust

The western movie is a seventy-five-year-long myth, as old as Hollywood cinema itself and to all the world the most spectacular achievement of the American motion picture industry.

How spectacular? Read the news. When the United States of America faces down its foes, it is not Uncle Sam against communist guerillas or masked terrorists; rather in our mind's eye it is a lone cowboy against all those hostiles out there, whether they resemble war-painted Cheyenne dog soldiers or slack-jawed bushwhackers and backshooters. More, when this eager republic finally assembles the hardware to launch another extraterrestrial expedition—and next time, Mars—it will not be understood as childlike technocrats swimming toward some rock-collecting expedition. Rather, it will be presented as gravelly-voiced pioneers blasting off to tame that high frontier in the stars.

Bluntly, modern America, raised at the movies, has costumed itself in the myth of the rough-riding, straight-shooting, and sunset-bound cowboy. He is frontier justice; he is whatever's right; he is the god who came to earth to make thunder in the dust. Who cannot laugh at the notion that America would not wish to be buried with a five-day stubble and its boots on?

What is going on here? America as a cowboy? During the first century of the republic, the face of America to the world was the image of the twin cataracts at Niagara Falls; during the second century, it was F. A. Bartholdi's Statue of Liberty in New York harbor. And yet now it is indisputable that the face America will offer throughout its third century is that of the cowboy. How has such an amazing transformation come about? And most curious of all, why should the most powerful and luxurious state in creation fancy itself parch-mouthed from the trail and ordering a shot of rub-of-the-brush at the Long Branch saloon?

The scout, Robert Mitchum, keeps watch on a lonely knoll.

How the West Was Completely Made Up

What tens of thousands of directors, writers, actors, and horses have done is most old and then again forever new. They have turned bald lies into classic set pieces and hamboned cameos into giants like the Ringo Kid in *Stagecoach* (1939), Thomas Dunson in *Red River* (1948), and Ethan Edwards in *The Searchers* (1956). Those greedy, ill-read, and bottomlessly American rascals one thinks of as Hollywood-and-God-Bless-It have discovered for themselves the profound strength in telling a completely make-believe story of heroes and maidens and destiny as if they were a single voice singing an epic memory of a golden age. And the members of the movie audience recognize what was never fact as if it were their own lives—as if they had always been riding a stagecoach through Apache country or waiting for the train at high noon to deliver a scar-faced killer to a frightened cowtown.

The western moviemakers have become bards just as surely as the western has become a song, an epiphany, a tragedy, and an opera.

"Yes he was truly born to entertain," says Ned (Burt Lancaster) Buntline of Buffalo Bill (Paul Newman) Cody, the first western showman, a one man proto-Hollywood, in Robert Altman's Buffalo Bill and the Indians *(1976). "No ordinary man would have had the foresight to take credit for acts of bravery and heroism that he couldn't have done. And no ordinary man could realize that tremendous profit could be made by telling a pack of lies in front of witnesses like it was* the truth. No, Bill Cody can only trust his senses, and when his senses fail him, he might just see things as they really are."

What is crucial is that all mankind's time-honored mythmakers happen all at once in the western movie. In seventy-five years, there have been over four thousand westerns produced, and to experience one or many or all is to witness a kaleidoscope of mankind's myths, one surmounting another in a breathless quoting, the moviemakers like willful children plundering every toy once-upon-a-time at Santa Claus's workshop.

That is not the western United States on the screen, stretched between the Mississippi River and California's Gold Coast. That is the *west*—a timeless never-never land of great expectations and grand illusions. In the western movie, Hamlet is just as likely to call himself Thomas Jefferson (James Stewart) Destry and aim to bring law and order to the corrupt Bottleneck in George Marshall's *Destry Rides Again* (1939) as Colonel George Armstrong (Errol Flynn) Custer, in Raoul Walsh's *They Died with Their Boots On* (1941), is to stand with his fringe coat flapping in the breeze like the Spartan King Leonidas fighting to the death with his men at the battle of Thermopylae. And more, westerns can quote westerns quoting myth, as in the first of John Ford's cavalry trilogy *Fort Apache* (1948). Here Colonel Owen (Henry Fonda) Thursday re-creates George (Errol Flynn) Custer re-creating Leonidas while giving a lesson of vainglory to Captain Kirby (John Wayne) York:

"We've dug in on the ridge, sir," says Captain Kirby (John Wayne) York in John Ford's Fort Apache *(1948), "plenty of water and ammunition." He points into the distance, trying to explain how he means to save the baggage train of the ambushed and doomed regiment. "I've sent a courier to Fort Grant, if we can only hold out. Here, get on my horse."*

The wounded, unarmed, and cooly desperate Colonel Owen (Henry Fonda) Thursday climbs up from the dust and onto York's stallion, replying, "I'll trouble you for your saber, Captain."

"My saber?"

"I must rejoin my command," insists Thursday.

York protests, "The command is wiped out and there's nothing we can do about it."

"I'm not asking your opinion Captain York. When you command this regiment, and you probably will, command it! Your saber sir. Any questions Captain?"

"No questions."

Later — in the second and third parts of Ford's cavalry trilogy, *She Wore a Yellow Ribbon* (1949) and *Rio Grande* (1950) — York will re-create Thursday, Custer, and Leonidas.

All this wondrous confusion of any culture's myths and no one's version of history is not only possible in the western, it is the igneous rockbed of the western movie. The cowboys, Indians, cavalrymen, and settlers on the screen seem to demand their lie be lied about too — a tall tale insisting it is taller than any other, western moviemakers boastfully standing on the shoulders of those Old World knights and monsters to howl Hallelujah, top this!

In John Ford's ironic law and order story, *The Man Who Shot Liberty Valance* (1962), there is a famous line about fact and fiction in the western movie: the intellectual editor of the *Shinbone Star* tears up the transcription of the so-called true story of the rise of Senator Ransom (James Stewart) Stoddard because it undercuts the town's notion of how innocent Stoddard gunned down the evil Liberty (Lee Marvin) Valance; the editor explains, "This is the West, when the fact becomes legend, print the legend!"

Yes, but then again, the editor is also a prankster: there are no facts to print. The western is most successful, and perhaps even most American, when it is most plagiaristic and out of bounds, when it does not even bother to wink about the facts of the case or where that crazy idea comes from. The western understands that the truth is too important to be left to newspapers and historians. What happened? The good guys won. Why did he go bad? He was a *varmit.* What is to be done? Go west. Where is the west? Wherever freedom lives.

"Wherever they go they'll be on my land," explains the cowboy Thomas (John Wayne) Dunson in Red River *(1948). "My land. We're here and we're going to stay here. Give me ten years and I'll have that brand on the gates of the greatest ranch in Texas. The big house will be down by the river and the corrals and the bunkhouse behind it. It'll be a good place to live in. Ten years and I'll have the Red River D on more cattle than you've ever looked at. I'll have that brand on enough beef to — to feed the whole country. Good beef for hungry people. Beef to make 'em strong, make 'em grow. It takes work, it takes sweat, it takes time, lots of time, lots of time."*

OPPOSITE: the misty calm of this dawn location in New Mexico belies the work it took to achieve it.

And then there is the final question, the most compelling, Why has America chosen the cowboy as a self-image? If these westerns are not histories but an encyclopedia of myth, if none of this landscape ever existed in time, nor none of these gun-slinging saddle tramps ever breathed hard and bellowed—as does Pike (William Holden) in *The Wild Bunch* (1969): "We're gonna stick together, just like it used to be. When you side with a man, you stay with him, and if you can't do that, you're like some animal, you're finished. We're finished! All of us! Mount up!"— then why should America want to side with a man, stand tall, draw fast, and sleep with its best pony near at hand?

The answer is the magic of the western, and it is in the magic of America. America invented itself: no bloodlines, no titled deeds, just genesis, declaring independence as if by wizardry, forming a more perfect union out of no union, guaranteeing life and liberty and then pursuing happiness without any mandate other than brash imagination and an itch.

As America began, so the western movie begins, out of nothing before it and with a spontaneous conceit of the mind: we are here, let the games begin—or, in Hollywood parlance, lights, camera, action!

The western movie is beginnings and about beginnings. That is the obsessive persuasion on the screen. There are no middles. There are no ends. That is why any myth will do, because all the western wants from it is the conception; and that is why the best sort of western is a quilt of the very beginnings of myths: winning the land, righting a wrong, slaying the savage beast, bringing law and order, all those big stampedes under big skies in the big country. As the cattle agent says in Howard Hawks's *Red River* (1948), "There're three times in a man's life when he's got a right to yell at the moon. When he marries, when his children come, and when he finishes a job he had to be crazy to start!"

The western movie is crazy to start and then to start again. It is ambition anew, vanity awakened, imagination erupted. Is it even flickeringly surprising that a nation of fanatics, misfits, land-grabbers, pensioned-off soldiers, bonded slaves, half-breed losers, and yearning immigrants should have a permanent appetite for eternal nativity?

And the cowboy? He is the Declaration of Independence, the Constitution, and the Bill of Rights all at once. His face is exactly the same that Niagara Falls and the Statue of Liberty offered in their time, with the significant and grandly fun amendment that the cowboy exists in motion amount. The cowboy of the western never entered history so he need never finish or die. The cowboy invents himself and also lifts our hearts with laughter each time he shouts, "Mount up!"

"Looks like I got the plague, don't it?" remarks the outlaw Ringo Kid (John Wayne) in John Ford's Stagecoach *(1939) when the other passengers shun him at the dinner table. "No," responds the gold-hearted whore Dallas (Claire Trevor), "that's not true."*

OPPOSITE: Jimmy Stewart, in *Two Rode Together*, travels through the wide open spaces that are quintessential cowboy country.

"Well," says Ringo, starting to move away, *"I guess you can't break out of prison and into society in the same week."*

———

"You shoot it out with them," begins the shrewd Thomas Jefferson (James Stewart) Destry in George Marshall's Destry Rides Again *(1939), "and for some reason or another, I don't know why, but they look like heroes. But you put 'em behind bars and they look little and cheap like they oughta look, and it serves as a warning for the rest of them to keep away."*

"That won't work here in Bottleneck," comments the former town drunk, who is now the earnest if impotent Bottleneck sheriff (Charles Winninger) and who has beckoned the son of the famous lawman Destry to come and help him clean up the town's corruption.

The young Destry continues, *"I'm gonna stay here and do this job I come for. My Pa did it the old way, and I'm gonna do it the new way, and if I don't do it right, I'll get*

out of town quick enough, don't worry. Come on, swear me in sheriff."*

———

"It's dis country dat got my boy killed, yes sir I—!"

"Now Lars," assures Ma (Olive Carey) Jorgenson in John Ford's The Searchers *(1956), "it just so happens we be Texicans. A Texican is nothing but a human man way out on a limb, this year and next, and maybe for a hundred more, but I don't think forever. Someday this country's gonna be a fine place to be, maybe it needs our bones in the ground before that time can come."* She stands and announces, *"Bedtime!"*

After she departs, her husband Lars (John Qualen) comments, *"She was a school teacher, you know."*

———

"All I know, Jim," says a horse thief (Randy Quaid) to a bushwhacker (Marlon Brando) in Arthur Penn's Missouri Breaks *(1976, screenplay by Thomas McGuane), "is that life is not like anything I ever seen before."*

OPPOSITE: virile and taciturn, the cowboy hero has the qualities of a solitary god who comes down from the hills to set wrong to right.

"Well," says the Ringo Kid (John Wayne) in John Ford's Stagecoach *(1939), "there are some things that a man just can't run away from."*

It took John Ford, John Wayne, Utah's Monument Valley, and the splendiferous *Stagecoach* (1939) to rescue the western from the crooning cowboys of the 1930s. *Stagecoach,* based on a Guy de Maupassant story, is both a traveling carnival of desire and a light-year jump into the landscape of myth. Both before and after, Ford made much of the historical detail in his copious, spiritually deft work. Yet one look at the imperial spires, mesas, and castellated crags of Monument Valley, hung with brooding nimbo-stratus clouds, or one hearing of stagedriver (Andy Devine) Buck's famous warning, "If there's anything I hate it's driving a stage through Apache country," or of Doc (Thomas Mitchell) Boone's operatic observation, "It's that old Apache butcher Geronimo—Geronimo, nice name for a butcher," and one knows that this is not an arcane episode of yesteryear but a panoramic and eternal pilgrimage—from childhood to manhood, from abandonment to nurture, through the valley of the shadow of death.

Stagecoach's Ringo Kid (John Wayne) is the centerpiece, regardless of how few lines he speaks, not only because he is the hero but also because he becomes America. Virile, innocent, ardent, brutish, heavily armed, laconic, and casually anti-intellectual—"I know all I need to know"—the Ringo Kid emerges from the lustrous sandstone and hoary sagebrush of Monu-

ment Valley, literally, and proceeds to lay waste to whatever's wrong. He is driven by passion both to revenge a crime against his own family and to conquer the future with sudden violence. A title would not change him, nor would a badge, wealth, misfortune, jail, the right or wrong woman, or a bullet with his name on it. This is not a psychologically astute man; this is a miracle of flesh, post-Fall but pre-Kingdom, what modern man longs to become if he could just escape gravity. The Ringo Kid is also a battleground of human paradoxes: the good man who kills, the outlaw who escapes, the lover who marries a whore, the survivor who routinely dares death. His outsized nature enfranchises the passengers on the stagecoach either to find the best in themselves or to destroy themselves. At the finish, when he shoots three bad men while actually flying forward into the dust, the only question is, why not three hundred? And when the marshal purposefully forgets to arrest him and permits the Ringo Kid to ride off to pursue happiness with his beloved whore, the emotional satisfaction is that associated with divine intervention. Arrest America? On what authority? And what would it matter? America is heroically free anywhere it goes, and wherever it goes, there becomes free.

"Hold it!" calls the Ringo Kid, saddle in one hand, spinning a Winchester rifle in the other, as he stops the stagecoach in the middle of Monument Valley.
"Whoa! Steady!" shouts stagedriver Buck to his team. "Whoa! Whoa! Hey look, it's Ringo!"

OPPOSITE: Indians line up at their campground, ready to turn themselves over to the U.S. Army, in an episode from John Ford's *Cheyenne Autumn,* 1964.

"Well," says Ringo, starting to move away, "I guess you can't break out of prison and into society in the same week."

━━━━━

"You shoot it out with them," begins the shrewd Thomas Jefferson (James Stewart) Destry in George Marshall's Destry Rides Again (1939), "and for some reason or another, I don't know why, but they look like heroes. But you put 'em behind bars and they look little and cheap like they oughta look, and it serves as a warning for the rest of them to keep away."

"That won't work here in Bottleneck," comments the former town drunk, who is now the earnest if impotent Bottleneck sheriff (Charles Winninger) and who has beckoned the son of the famous lawman Destry to come and help him clean up the town's corruption.

The young Destry continues, "I'm gonna stay here and do this job I come for. My Pa did it the old way, and I'm gonna do it the new way, and if I don't do it right, I'll get out of town quick enough, don't worry. Come on, swear me in sheriff."

━━━━━

"It's dis country dat got my boy killed, yes sir I—!"

"Now Lars," assures Ma (Olive Carey) Jorgenson in John Ford's The Searchers (1956), "it just so happens we be Texicans. A Texican is nothing but a human man way out on a limb, this year and next, and maybe for a hundred more, but I don't think forever. Someday this country's gonna be a fine place to be, maybe it needs our bones in the ground before that time can come." She stands and announces, "Bedtime!"

After she departs, her husband Lars (John Qualen) comments, "She was a school teacher, you know."

━━━━━

"All I know, Jim," says a horse thief (Randy Quaid) to a bushwhacker (Marlon Brando) in Arthur Penn's Missouri Breaks (1976, screenplay by Thomas McGuane), "is that life is not like anything I ever seen before."

OPPOSITE: virile and taciturn, the cowboy hero has the qualities of a solitary god who comes down from the hills to set wrong to right.

In the beginning of beginnings was the hero, and it is one true joy that the reign of the western has obliged almost every memorable movie actor to play at cowboy or cowgirl, including Charles Laughton, Spencer Tracy, and Sophia Loren. Only Laurence Olivier seems to have escaped, with the note that the zest of his movie *Henry V* (1944) owes less to Shakespeare than to the cavalry riding to the rescue.

In the silent westerns, the hero's name was William S. Hart, Tom Mix, Harry Carey, Hoot Gibson, Colonel Tim McCoy, Yakima Canutt; but the greatest of these was Tom Mix. He was a self-described outrage, dressing himself like a bleached Christmas tree and touring America in order to "give 'em a reel outta one of my pictures." He was said to ride his white horse into the huge barroom in Los Angeles where all the cowboy extras hung out while making movies; he would wave his hat and shout, "Tom Mix, boys, the drinks are on me!"

Harry Carey had his legion of fans too, the two most significant being John Ford and John Wayne. It would be Ford who developed a gritty style for the silent western. After the box office success of James Cruze's epic *The Covered Wagon* (1923), Ford gained license to try the sweeping, studio-rattling *The Iron Horse* (1924), a story about the building of the Union Pacific railroad that was so muscular that the shooting locations are said to have featured 200-proof bootleg whiskey and so many fights in the mess hall that they

had to take the ketchup bottles off the tables. The last epic silent western was Henry King's *The Winning of Barbara Worth* (1926) about the settling of California's Imperial Valley. Shot in Oregon through wild rain and wind, it features a flood set-piece that compares favorably to the book of Genesis and dwarfs anything tried since.

Talkies ended the amateurish careers of the genuine cowhands who had come down to Hollywood to drink with Tom Mix; the depression after 1929 greatly frightened the studios away from financing the out-of-doors locations primary to the magic of the westerns. After all, the American landscape—purple mountains' majesty, amber waves of grain—is a full-fledged character in the western; without real sunrises and sunsets, the western is no more than a cramped soundstage where bold dialogue rings wrong-headed. And when Raoul Walsh's lavish sound epic *The Big Trail* (1930) failed badly at the box office—stunting the rookie career of wavy-haired John Wayne—Hollywood seemed justified in its penny-pinching, which continued despite Wesley Ruggles's money-making out-of-door land rush epic *Cimmaron* (1931). In retrospect, it is fair to say that Hollywood was only reflecting the profound fear and hopelessness that suffocated America in the 1930s. If the western is a clean slate upon which America writes its wishes, then the western's retreat to dingy sets and feckless fantasy during the depression is sad, scary evidence of an American nightmare.

Gregory Peck strides along purposefully in *Billy Two Hats,* 1974. OPPOSITE: two pros, John Wayne and Robert Mitchum, team up for *El Dorado,* 1967.

It took John Ford, John Wayne, Utah's Monument Valley, and the splendiferous *Stagecoach* (1939) to rescue the western from the crooning cowboys of the 1930s. *Stagecoach,* based on a Guy de Maupassant story, is both a traveling carnival of desire and a light-year jump into the landscape of myth. Both before and after, Ford made much of the historical detail in his copious, spiritually deft work. Yet one look at the imperial spires, mesas, and castellated crags of Monument Valley, hung with brooding nimbo-stratus clouds, or one hearing of stagedriver (Andy Devine) Buck's famous warning, "If there's anything I hate it's driving a stage through Apache country," or of Doc (Thomas Mitchell) Boone's operatic observation, "It's that old Apache butcher Geronimo—Geronimo, nice name for a butcher," and one knows that this is not an arcane episode of yesteryear but a panoramic and eternal pilgrimage—from childhood to manhood, from abandonment to nurture, through the valley of the shadow of death.

Stagecoach's Ringo Kid (John Wayne) is the centerpiece, regardless of how few lines he speaks, not only because he is the hero but also because he becomes America. Virile, innocent, ardent, brutish, heavily armed, laconic, and casually anti-intellectual—"I know all I need to know"—the Ringo Kid emerges from the lustrous sandstone and hoary sagebrush of Monu-

ment Valley, literally, and proceeds to lay waste to whatever's wrong. He is driven by passion both to revenge a crime against his own family and to conquer the future with sudden violence. A title would not change him, nor would a badge, wealth, misfortune, jail, the right or wrong woman, or a bullet with his name on it. This is not a psychologically astute man; this is a miracle of flesh, post-Fall but pre-Kingdom, what modern man longs to become if he could just escape gravity. The Ringo Kid is also a battleground of human paradoxes: the good man who kills, the outlaw who escapes, the lover who marries a whore, the survivor who routinely dares death. His outsized nature enfranchises the passengers on the stagecoach either to find the best in themselves or to destroy themselves. At the finish, when he shoots three bad men while actually flying forward into the dust, the only question is, why not three hundred? And when the marshal purposefully forgets to arrest him and permits the Ringo Kid to ride off to pursue happiness with his beloved whore, the emotional satisfaction is that associated with divine intervention. Arrest America? On what authority? And what would it matter? America is heroically free anywhere it goes, and wherever it goes, there becomes free.

"Hold it!" calls the Ringo Kid, saddle in one hand, spinning a Winchester rifle in the other, as he stops the stagecoach in the middle of Monument Valley.

"Whoa! Steady!" shouts stagedriver Buck to his team. "Whoa! Whoa! Hey look, it's Ringo!"

OPPOSITE: Indians line up at their campground, ready to turn themselves over to the U.S. Army, in an episode from John Ford's *Cheyenne Autumn,* 1964.

"Yeah," growls Marshal (George Bancroft) Curly, who is riding shotgun in pursuit of the jail-breaking Ringo Kid; he adds, "Hello Kid."

"Hello Curly," says Ringo. "Hiya Buck, how's your folks?"

"Oh, just fine Ringo, except my grandfather come down—"

"Shut up," snaps Marshal Curly.

The Ringo Kid says, "Didn't expect to see you riding shotgun on this run, Marshal."

"Goin' to Loresburg? I figured you'd be there by this time," says Marshal Curly, who knows Ringo has broken out of jail to avenge his family against the evil Luke Plummer in Loresburg.

"No," says Ringo, "lame horse. Well, it looks like you've got another passenger."

"Yeah," says Marshal Curly, aiming his shotgun, "I'll take the Winchester."

"You may need me and this Winchester, Curly," says Ringo, referring to the Apache threat. "Saw a ranch house burnin' last night."

"You don't understand, Kid," counters Marshal Curly, "you're under arrest."

"Curly," begins Ringo, considering a fight; but then he spies a cavalry escort coming up from behind and surrenders his weapon by ejecting the shell in the magazine. He climbs into the stage cabin, saying, "Hope I ain't crowdin' you folks none."

The six passengers (doctor, banker, gambler, drummer, pregnant lady, whore) respond, "No, more the merrier."

As the stage accelerates, the corrupt banker Gatewood (Benton Churchill) scoffs, "So you're the notorious Ringo Kid."

Ringo responds easily, "My friends just call me Ringo—nickname I had as a kid. Right name's Henry."

"Seems to me I knew your family, Henry," remarks the good-natured Doc Boone. "Didn't I fix your arm once when you were, oh, bumped off a horse?"

"Are you Doc Boone?" asks Ringo.

"I certainly am. Now let's see. I'd just been honorably discharged from the Union Army—after the war of the rebellion."

"You mean the war for the southern confederacy," corrects the gambler Hatfield (John Carradine)

"I mean nothing of the kind, sir."

"That was my kid brother who broke his arm," continues Ringo. "You did a good job, Doc, even if you was drunk."

"Thank you, son," nods Doc Boone. "Professional compliments are always pleasing. What happened to that boy whose arm I fixed?"

Ringo darkens and replies, "He was murdered."

After the Ringo Kid, each cowboy hero had two choices: he could stretch or shave the prototype. Or he could doubt the worthiness of his own mantle, even though the audience knew intrinsically that this saddlebum was more splendid than even he recognized. The Ringo Kid even made the villain's work easier. To defy the Ringo Kid was to be bad unto death.

John Wayne chased his own original fate the rest of his career, and it is a measure of his personal success that the more he triumphed on the screen, both the larger the mythological landscape of the western became and the sharper the intellectual resistance to him grew in the nation he embodied. The fault was not in him, true, it was in the stars and stripes. He could not change; he was a god; he was Achilles. Meanwhile, the best part of America yearned to change—to grow up, from an isolationist bumpkin to a mature state; to learn to nurture, emerging from an adolescent backwater to a

Charlton Heston—who has been called Hollywood's "resident epic hero"—brought his usual determined strength to *Will Penny*, 1968.

loving home of orphaned peoples.

Then again, history needs myth more than vice versa, and for four generations of American children, John Wayne kept coming, gun in hand, like mother nature except taller in the saddle. When he charged that Japanese pillbox in Allan Dwan's *The Sands of Iwo Jima* (1944), the Ringo Kid, playing the indestructible Sergeant John (John Wayne) Stryker, told America it could whip the Axis. When he, playing the ambitious Thomas (John Wayne) Dunson, held forth the most stirring soliloquy in western movies in Howard Hawks's *Red River* (1948), the Ringo Kid told the world it could recover from the horror of the second world war. And when he, playing the inexorable Ethan (John Wayne) Edwards, searched for Emily (Natalie Wood) Edwards beyond reason in the greatest western extant, John Ford's *The Searchers* (1956), who could not understand that the relentless Ringo Kid would never quit until the world was set straight, and that if you did not let America save you, it might just destroy you in the attempt.

"Well, we start tomorrow," begins Thomas (John Wayne) Dunson to his wranglers on the eve of the cattle drive in Howard Hawks's Red River *(1948). "We're going to Missouri with ten thousand head. Most of you men have come back to Texas from the war. You came back to nothing. You found your homes gone, your cattle scattered and your land stolen by carpetbaggers. Well there's no money and no work because there's no market for beef in the south, but there is in Missouri. So we're goin' to Missouri. . . . Cumberland didn't make it. No one else has. That's the reason I'm here. I want you all to know what you're up against. You probably already know, but I want to make sure you do. We've got a thousand miles to go. Ten miles a day'll be good, fifty'll be luck. It will be dry country, dry wells when we get to 'em. There'll be wind and rain. There's gonna be Indian territory. How bad I don't know, and when we get to Missouri there'll be border gangs. It's gonna be a fight all the way, but we'll get there. Nobody has to come along. There'll still be a job for you when we get back. But remember this. Everybody who signs on for this drive agrees to finish it. There'll be no quittin' along the way. Not by me and not by you. Well, there's no hard feelings if you don't want to go, but just let me know."*

———

"Captain?" starts Ethan (John Wayne) Edwards as he rambles into the farmhouse kitchen near the beginning of John Ford's The Searchers *(1956). Finally returned to Texas from the Civil War, he has been awakened by a posse of Texas Rangers on the trail of what they think are cattle rustlers but are actually homicidal Indians. He is grumpily disrespectful to his old friend as he continues, "Captain the Reverend Samuel Johnson Clayton. Mighty impressive."*

"The prodigal brother," responds Captain the Reverend (Ward Bond) Clayton, equally mockingly, "when you'd get back? I ain't seen you since the surrender. Come to think of it, I didn't see you at the surrender."

"Don't believe in surrenderin'," counters Ethan Edwards. "Nope, I still got my saber, Reverend. Didn't turn it into no plow share neither."

John Wayne, the archetypal cowboy hero, is backed by the wide open desert of the mythic west in the all-time great western, John Ford's *The Searchers*, 1956.

Wild Indians in the western represent everything Grendel might have been had he understood light cavalry tactics and George Armstrong Custer. Recall the saga of the Norse hero Beowulf, who was beckoned to the court of King Hrothgar to rid it of the marauding monster Grendel. Recall too how Grendel, "this cruel spirit, the fell and fen his fastness was, the march his haunt . . . ," — how this Grendel would come past nightfall to invade the court and slaughter great numbers, so that he "became ruler; against right he fought, one against all," and so that "empty then stood the best of houses" as Grendel's "dark death-shadow drove always against them, old and young."

The western's wild Indian is this frightening and worse! For not only could he come from out of the wilderness like a spectre to slaughter — for no reason, because like Grendel he was cast out of Heaven as a kindred of Cain — but also, in order to calm their fears, cowboy heroes often tell settlers that the Indians will not attack, like Grendel, at night. Not at night? Since these struggles have no bearing in fact, why not? Because it would have been too terrible! The actors on the screen and the audiences in the theater could not have endured the cataclysm of terror Grendel's victims at Hrothgar's court suffered.

"Stealin' the cattle was just to pull us out," comments Ethan (John Wayne) Edwards to the Reverend Samuel John-

son (Ward Bond) Clayton in John Ford's The Searchers *(1956) when he and their Texas Ranger posse find a stolen bull that has been wastefully slaughtered by Indian raiders deep inside Monument Valley. "This is a murder raid," adds Ethan Edwards; he turns to Lars (John Qualen) Jorgenson. "Shapes up to either your place or — my brother's."*

Settler Lars Jorgenson cries, "Glory, oh please, God, please no!" He calls, "Brad, Brad, son!"

Captain Clayton summarizes, "Jorgenson's place is the closest, Ethan. If they're not there, we'll come straight on to you. Come on, Charley!"

Meanwhile, back at the Edwards' homestead, Father Aaron (Walter Coy) and Mother Martha (Dorothy Jordan) Edwards have already spotted the signs on the landscape that the murder raid is coming against them and their three children. They have boarded the windows and are preparing to hand out their youngest daughter Emily (Natalie Wood) through the back window to hide in the graveyard in the back.

Aaron Edwards says, "Hurry up Martha, the moon's fixin' to rise."

Martha instructs little Emily, "You won't make a sound or come back no matter what you hear. Promise?"

"I promise." Yet Emily resists a moment. "Wait, can't I have Topsy?"

"There's no time," protests Aaron.

Martha fetches the rag doll and hands it over. "Here she is baby, here."

Aaron lifts Emily out the window, adding, "Down! Low! Run!"

Martha cries what will be a goodbye forever, "Baby!"

Significantly, those are no more historical Native Americans on the screen than Grendel was some particular man or beast. That is not the plain tragedy of racial bigotry up there, either, though in the worst of western movie writing,

The "red Indian" is as essential to the western as the cowboy and just as much a creation of Hollywood mythmaking. OPPOSITE: Apache Indians in *Rio Conchos*. The Apache were the fiercest and most troublesome tribe in the Hollywood version of the west.

there is the stink of white supremacy. Rather, in the best of the corpus, the Indian is the nightmare you wake from, the shadow in the dim-lit kitchen when the wind howls, the irrational alien other who is coming for you, personally, from out of the dark and under your bed—the red boogeyman, who in American mythology replaced the Big Bad Wolf of European folklore. Just compare the Russian proverb, "Make yourself into a sheep, and you'll meet a wolf nearby," with the archetypal western movie proverb, "The only good Injun is a dead Injun."

More, wild Indians are most useful for mythmaking when they demonstrate Shakespearean proportions of cruelty, lust, and vengefulness. For the western to work on an epic scale, Indians cannot be nomadic hunter-gatherers; rather they must become roaming murder bands, screaming rapists, depraved warriors so sadistic at torture that neither the hero nor the camera can bear to look too closely at the staked-out, skinned, scalped, roasted, emasculated, or ravished victim.

"What you saw wasn't Lucy," admits Ethan Edwards to Brad (Harry Carey, Jr.) Jorgenson in John Ford's The Searchers *(1956). They have been tracking the Indian raiding party in pursuit of the kidnapped Edwards' girls Lucy and Emily. Brad has just reported that he has spotted the Indian raiding party camp over the ridge and that his beloved Lucy, the older Edwards daughter, is a hostage among them.*

"Oh, but it was I tell you!" protests Brad.

Ethan Edwards reluctantly confesses what he has kept from Brad for days. "What you saw was a buck wearin'

Lucy's dress. I found Lucy back in the canyon. Wrapped her in my coat—buried her with my own hands. Thought it best to keep it from you."

Brad is shattered, but must ask, "Did they? Was she—"

"What do you want me to do?" barks Ethan Edwards. "Draw you a picture? Spell it out? Don't ever ask me! Long as you live, don't ever ask me more!"

Repeatedly, the Indian tribes elected to Grendel's throne are the Apaches, the Commanches, the Cheyennes, the Sioux, the Kiowa, and, sometimes, the Blackfeet and Crow. Yet the Tom Mix and John Wayne of Indians was the Apache, often led by the historical war chiefs Cochise and Geronimo.

The facts of Cochise and Geronimo do not signify; their individual biographies are profound stories of the fall and desecration of the Native American in the face of unironic American progress. What the Apache of the westerns came to portray was the most virile, most angry, undefeated, unreconciled, unrepentant, and stoically bloody-minded human surrogates imaginable—so outlandishly fierce that to fight the Apache was to aggrandize oneself, to best him was to certify one's masculinity without in the least qualifying his noble savagery. As a listener of Grendel's tale must come to venerate the passion of the monster, so a witness to the western's war against the Apache must come to love so grand an illusion. And surely it is supremely ironic in respect both to the movie Apache and to the ghost of the historical Apache that when the 82nd All American and 101st Screaming

OPPOSITE: Indian raiders ride down a steep butte in Monument Valley, Utah.

Eagle airborne divisions jumped into fire and death over Normandy in June 1944, the troopers are said to have cried out as they had been taught, "Geronimo!"

"We here have little chance for glory or advancement," observes the frustrated and, because he is newly arrived, ill-informed Colonel Owen (Henry Fonda) Thursday to his officers in the first of John Ford's cavalry trilogy, Fort Apache *(1948). "While some of our brother officers are leading their well-publicized campaigns against the great Indian nations, the Sioux and the Cheyenne, we are asked to ward off the gnat stains and flea bites of a few cowardly digger Indians."*

"Your pardon, Colonel," counters the veteran Indian fighter Captain Kirby (John Wayne) York, "I would hardly call the Apache digger Indians."

Thursday reacts impatiently. "You'd scarcely compare them with the Sioux, Captain."

"No, I don't," agrees York. "The Sioux once raided into Apache territory. Old-timers told me you could follow their line of retreat from the bones of their dead."

"I suggest the Apache have deteriorated since then," protests Thursday, "judging by a few of the specimens I've seen on the way out here."

"Well," concludes York, "if you saw them, sir, they weren't Apaches."

The major exception to the overlordship of the Apache is the episode of the Sioux war chief Sitting Bull and his destruction of George Armstrong Custer and elements of the Seventh Cavalry Regiment at the Little Big Horn river, June 25, 1876. Yes, it happened and within spitting distance of the American centennial. But no, it was not even vaguely like all the Holly-

wood versions. Sitting Bull is presented as the leader of a shattering horde of warriors, so that when his teeming thousands massacre Custer, the drama moves past a dusty combat toward what must be regarded as a Wagnerian opera of promise and warning.

Sitting Bull's Sioux also become the blind fury of a mysterious, destructive universe. Only the power of mankind's myth can face off such a threat. Accordingly, in the greatest of the Custer movies, Raoul Walsh's *They Died with Their Boots On* (1941), Errol Flynn, the swashbuckling equivalent of John Wayne, pursues his destiny not like the Ringo Kid but like Prince Hal of *Henry IV*, a randy-eyed, misogynistic, self-doubting peacock of a campaigner, part in love with his enemies and all in love with himself. Nevertheless, when it comes time to stand and die for his country, Errol Flynn's Custer grows to *Henry V* proportions and launches boldly into chaos. Further, it cannot be a coincidence that Walsh's version of the hallowed battleground resembles a sandy beach on the English Channel at Dunkirk. And no matter what the version of the tale, Custer does not simply die, pierced by fate's arrows; rather he sacrifices himself to demonstrate that as tough as the monsters are, faithful, mortal, lion-hearted America is a fair equal, that no blood-price will be too high nor battle-shirt too heavy.

And is it an accident of history, or some jest by a perverse comic writer in Heaven, that the western movie enjoyed its glorious growth in color from the second world war to the Viet-

Indians lie in ambush, waiting for the call to "action."

nam war, when the color red symbolized fear, Armageddon, and an end to life as Hollywood knows it?

"Colonel, if you send out the regiment," complains Captain York to Colonel Thursday in John Ford's Fort Apache *(1948), "Cochise will think that I've tricked him."*

"Exactly," says Thursday. "We have tricked him, tricked him into returning to American soil, and I intend to see that he stays here."

York protests, "Colonel Thursday, I gave my word to Cochise. No man is going to make a liar out of me, sir."

"Your word to a breech-clothed savage? An illiterate uncivilized murderer and treaty breaker? There's no question of honor, sir, between an American officer and Cochise."

And much later, when the regiment is drawn up against the vast might of Cochise's Apache warriors in Monument Valley, Colonel Thursday rides forward to parley face to face with Cochise. Cochise proclaims in Spanish (the Indian is rarely given a voice, and when he does speak it is always in an undecipherable tongue or in broken English); he states his intentions to return to the reservation only if his people are guaranteed decent treatment by the corrupt Indian Agency and Washington.

Thursday rises from his campaign stool and roars, "Are you threatening me? I'll not sit here and be threatened. Beaufort, no preliminary nonsense with him, no ceremonial phrasing, straight from the shoulder as I tell you, do you hear?" Thursday raises his hand in anger. "They're recalcitrant swine and must feel it!"

Translator Sergeant Beaufort tries, "He's only speaking the truth, sir."

Thursday explodes, "Is there anyone in this regiment who understands an order when I give it!"

Beaufort relents, "What does the colonel wish me to say, sir?"

"Tell him I find him without honor," fires Thursday as Beaufort translates simultaneously. "Tell him they're not talking to me but to the United States government. Tell him that the government orders him to return to the reservation. And tell him if they've not started by dawn, we will attack! Tell him that!"

―――――

"He looks so small, Major," says a soldier, looking at the corpse of the slain Apache war chief Sierra (Michael Pete) Charriba in Sam Peckinpah's Major Dundee *(1964).*

Major (Charlton Heston) Dundee replies, "He was big enough once, son."

The United States Cavalry, at the movies, bears Beowulf's burden easily. The cavalry parades as front-fighters and sons of front-fighters and rises in dense escort to carouse like hellions. But when they must break the red trolls, they declaim, with Beowulf, "I abjure utterly the bearing of swords or shielding yellow board in this battle! With bare hands shall I grapple with the fiend, fight to the death here, hater and hated!"

Again, the facts of the Indian Wars, 1870–1895, do not signify; the Department of Defense admits to one thousand soldiers killed in action in twenty-five years. One thousand? Surely all those massacres must have wrecked more. But no, only at the movies. Also, the westerns make much of the actual military hardware of the cavalry—they did possess the Spencer, Henry, and Winchester repeating rifles, three-inch field artillery pieces, excellent quarter horses, and the famous Gatling gun. Yet it is as predictable as sunset that when the movie cavalry closes with the Indians, they will unsheath anachronistic sabers and leap from horse to ground to wrestle hand to hand with the foe. For that is not some historical military campaign on the screen; that is a battle between good and evil, between creation and destruction.

Further, what happens in a cavalry western is not the taming of the west, nor the bringing of law and order, nor anything like the horror of true war. Rather, the cavalry rides not to kill but *to rescue*. The innocent are snatched back from the jaws of the monster, the land is redeemed from the wicked, America itself is saved when Colonel Kirby (John Wayne) York, in John Ford's *Rio Grande* (1950), announces the attack against the Apache village to rescue kidnapped children, "Bugler sound charge . . . Follow me!"

And why does America need rescuing again and again? Why the cavalry, those dog-faced heroes in blue shirts (as John Ford's scripts call them), those fifty-cents-a-day professionals? The answer might be simple enough to explain American foreign policy from Teddy Roosevelt to the present. The U.S. Cavalry, and the U.S. Marines who serve as worthy modern surro-

gates, are proof to the audience of a loving God. When all else appears to have failed, when the wolf is in the house and the heart is in the throat, God will not forget you, the angel of death will walk the earth, David will slay his tens of thousands, and the cavalry will sound that charge and get there.

"This is a story you will tell your grandchildren, and mightily bored they will be," proclaims General (Edward Fox) Frost in Joseph E. Levine's A Bridge Too Far *(1977). Frost is addressing the officers of the British XXX Corps as they prepare to launch the ground attack through the German lines that was meant to link up three paratroop divisions dropped behind enemy lines in the daring, historical, and soon-to-fail Allied operation to strike from the Normandy beachheads all the way across the Rhine River in the summer of 1944, trying to end the European war in weeks rather than months.*

". . . Now, gentlemen, I'm not saying that this will be the easiest party that we've ever attended, but I still wouldn't miss it for the world. I like to think of this as one of those American western films. The paratroops, lacking substantial equipment, always short of food, these are the besieged homesteaders. The Germans, well naturally they're the bad guys. And Thirty Corps, we, my friends, are the cavalry — on the way to the rescue!"

The call of the bugle rouses the cavalry. Opposite: in a western, the cavalry comes not to kill but to rescue.

Fear of Women, Love of Boys, Men without Top Guns

The female is the harmless guest of the western movie, or is she? She is rarely afforded the self-destruction of Ophelia, and certainly never permitted the cherished Eve's role of Lady Macbeth. It is tempting to argue that the female is propped up as some sort of petticoated and frayed-haired Helen, but even this would be too convenient.

No, the female of mythology is too mysterious and potent a creature to let loose amongst those heavily armed and horse-happy cowboys, redmen, and troopers. The western prefers patience, charity, constancy, and unambiguous chastity. The western movie female is heavily clothed, her hair stuffed beneath a bonnet, her shawl wrapped tight on rounded shoulders, with a ladle or broom or child in hand. As a heroine, she is occasionally allowed on a horse; yet when she does mount up, wearing pants, there had best be some irregular detail, like an overlarge shirt or jacket, a ribbon on the pony tail, breasts overwhelming shoulders, or at least strident hygiene—fashioned for contrast to the dust.

"Now there's gonna be women with this column," says Sergeant (Victor McLaglen) Quinncannon in John Ford's She Wore a Yellow Ribbon *(1949), "and I want you men to watch them words—watch them words!"*

There were careful exceptions in the westerns of the 1970s, when the frontier woman was presented as grittier than her confused consort. At the time, this was considered feminist demythologizing. Yet at this remove, the heroines look more coy than contravening. Those soot-faced female survivors are best understood as a match to Clint Eastwood's version of the Ringo Kid—that self-centered coper who squinted his way through his so-called spaghetti westerns (made by Sergio Leone) in the 1960s and then was transformed by the naked violence of the Vietnam war into the ghostly avenger of Eastwood's own superb 70s and 80s westerns.

No matter the decade then, the female prototype of womb resplendent remained intact. After all, the western female is not on camera for action; she is ripe for reaction. To flirt with, to honor, to ravage, rescue, marry, or best of all, to leave. And if her name is something comportable like Annie, Sue Ellen, or Mrs. anything, there is cohesion, though better still is Mary or Marion. For while the best of the corpus piously acknowledges God the Father as justice itself, there is a coterminous desire to lug the cult of the Virgin west in those prairie schooners. Consider how the female is always propped up like statues at the Circus Maximus, stiff with fear yet also wide-eyed at that ceaseless Greco-Roman wrestling for whatever's right.

"Can I give you a hand?" asks Cole (Gary Cooper) Harden in William Wyler's The Westerner *(1940), as he glides into the homestead kitchen.*

"Oh no, thanks," responds Sue Ellen (Doris Davenport) Matthews, who is cleaning dishes at the sink. Her father has pleaded with her to try to convince the cowboy Cole Harden to

A pioneer woman, silhouetted in her characteristic bonnet, faces whatever the west has in store.

In the western, the faces of girls as well as women are likely to be lined with what can only be called frontier stoicism.

stay on at the homestead to help with the harvest; more important, Sue Ellen fancies Cole, and he is not unaware of her beauty. She adds, "Won't you sit down, please?"

"Well, I won't argue with you," Cole jokes. "If I had to wash dishes, I guess I'd give up eatin'."

"What do you do about dishes when you're home?"

"Home? You mean in a house?"

"You live in a house, don't you?"

"No." Cole casts his eyes. "No, my house is all out there. All one room, with a sky for a roof."

"Well—" Sue Ellen smiles with some puzzlement, adding, "Big place."

"Got some space to rent."

"Oh," Sue Ellen blinks. "I guess California is your next stop?"

"California." Cole nods. "But I don't stop. Oregon next I guess."

"Oh, uh, all places are just the same," tries Sue Ellen. "Wouldn't you rather stay a little longer in some places?"

"No, they're all the same. Beautiful when you leave 'em. It's, well, it's like the turtles. Carry their houses with 'em. If I had to build me a house, well I'd have it on wheels."

"Not me," Sue Ellen asserts. "I'd want my house so that nothing could ever move it. So down deep that an earthquake couldn't shake it and a cyclone would be just another wind going by."

"Well," returns Cole, very uneasily, "you say who wants to be a turtle. And I say, I hope you'll be very happy in your house." He turns to retreat. "Well—"

Sue Ellen starts, "Oh, say, wait a minute."

"What?"

"I know something we could agree on."

Cole is taken. "What's that?"

"In about a week now we're going to husk the corn." Sue Ellen beams. "And I'll bet you'll agree that's fun."

Cole is dumbfounded. "Huh?"

Sue Ellen presses, "Well, I'll bet you'd agree husking corn is the greatest fun in the world."

"Husking corn—fun?"

"Oh yes!" cries Sue Ellen.

"Well," says Cole, straining not to mock, "I'd rather wash dishes."

"Oh, no," sighs Sue Ellen.

"Well, it was a fine supper," says Cole, stepping to the door, "good cookin'."

Sue Ellen's father appears in the window, waving at her to try harder. Sue Ellen gathers her courage and starts, "Oh, Mr. Harden?"

"Huh?"

Sue Ellen swallows hard and tries a smile, bursting out blushingly, "What a handsome man you are."

Cole freezes, blushes in return, looks at the floor, then mumbles, "Well, I doubt that but—I'm a tired one. I, uh, hope I see you in the morning—before I leave."

Sue Ellen's gambit is complete when the next scene reveals the morning, with her and Cole riding horses close together through the cornfields.

The dance hall queen and cathouse whore provide the left hand to the chaste right of the western movie female. Most of the great movie femme fatales have been drafted to the role— Mae West, Marlene Dietrich, Betty Grable, Joan Crawford, Marilyn Monroe, Shelley Winters, Jean Seberg, Brigitte Bardot, Claudia Cardinale, Julie Christie—not for their considerable beauty but because the heart of gold that the role must possess also requires articulate gusto to make it shine. The fallen woman is the cowboy's only true human oasis; she is the female character he can always turn to for adoration

and tell her, tell her everything's all right, and there aren't any more guns in the valley."

"Shane," calls Joey, seeing the wound, "it's bloody, you're hurt."

"I'm all right, Joey. You go home to your mother and father, and grow up to be strong and straight. And Joey, take care of 'em, both of them."

"Yes, Shane," says Joey, realizing he is losing his plea; he adds about the backshooter, "He'd never been able to shoot you if you'da seen him."

Shane is riding away and calls, "Goodbye, little Joe."

Joey is still dealing with his memory of the gunfight. "He'd never even have cleared the holster, would he, Shane?" Joey sees Shane riding away; he starts after him, pleading, "Pa's got things for you to do, and Mother wants you, I know she does." Joey runs some more, crying, "Shane! Shane! Come back!" Joey weeps and adds, "Goodbye, Shane!"

Men without top guns, such as the homesteader Joe Start, serve like telegraph lines between the cowboy and the west he aims to tame. Indian scouts, stagecoach drivers, barkeeps, chuckwagon sages, impotent town sheriffs, farmers, sheepherders, undertakers, barbers, newspaper editors, cavalry sergeants and lieutenants, and wheezing sidekicks—the most famous being Gabby Hayes, Walter Brennan, Slim Pickens, Jay Silverheels, Victor McLaglen, Ward Bond, Ben Johnson, Hank Worden, Noah Beery, Jr., Woody Strode, Jack Elam—provide humor, clues, applause, and the often chewy proverb to keep the cowboy on course.

"Plantin' and readin', plantin' and readin'," groans a cowpoke (Hank Worden) in Howard Hawks's Red River

(1948) after Thomas (John Wayne) Dunson has gunned down another foe. "Fill a man full of lead, stick him in the ground and then read words over him. Why, when you kill a man, why try to read the Lord as a partner on the job?"

Most curious of all men without top guns is the western movie Negro. He is usually little regarded, yet almost always presented as out of bondage. The western wants it both ways, ignoring and restoring the black man, an ambivalence that imitates America's. And given that the western is not an historical document, it could have reached much farther to assert the 13th Amendment that so many of the western heroes are said to have fought for.

"Jethro?" calls Jim (Richard Widmark) Bowie to his slave on the eve of the final battle in John Wayne's The Alamo *(1960).*

The aged Jethro approaches. "Yes, sir?"

"This is something I, uh, promised Mrs. Bowie." Bowie hands up a piece of paper and asks, "Know what it is?"

Jethro looks at the paper he can clearly not read. "No, sir."

"That's your freedom. You're a free man, Jeth."

"Thank you, sir," says Jethro somberly.

"You better get your belongings together and get on over the wall tonight," says Bowie, gesturing into the dark. "It's gonna be more than a little rough around here. Good luck, Jeth."

"Thank you, sir." Jeth starts away, then turns back, asking, "Uh, Colonel Bowie, you say I'm a free man?"

"That's right."

"Well, if I'm free, then I got a right to decide what I'm gonna do. That's what you men are fightin' for." Jethro nods to himself with satisfaction and resolve, closing, "So, I reckon I'll—I'll stay."

OPPOSITE: ex-pro football player Jim Brown makes his movie debut as a soldier in the post-Civil War western *Rio Conchos*, 1964.

As big as the American west is, the western movies take such an enormous landscape and mold it into another planet. And what does this planet west look like? There is one blazing sun, but no finite horizon, so one assumes that it is flat and bordered by fire. There is one moon, and it is usually fixing to rise. The days are long, hot, dry, windy, and well-lit; the nights are short, cold, wet, noisy, and rarely starry (the camera does not look up). Up is the Oregon Territory, Wyoming, Montana, boot hill, and some icy place called Alaska. Down is Texas, the Rio Grande, and Mexico. The Devil lives in Texas and rents out the Arizona Territory, and Texas is said to be bigger than the planet. Back east is Boston, Philadelphia, Washington (New York is unspeakable), and beyond those frail places and across some meaningless ocean there is a dandified, unnamed continent of snooty weaklings and drunken Shakespearean actors. The South, now vanished, once consisted of "Virginie" and Georgia, both of which were razed to ashes by Yankee devils. Out west is California, the sunset, or, better yet, the gold strike.

The planet west has ponderous geography: a wandering desert dominated by pitchfork-shaped cactuses; a colossal mountain range with snow-filled passes or tricky, secret ravines; rivers so broad they resemble lakes or so fast they create breakers; and forests that start suddenly and peter out on hillsides. The prairie stretches hither to yon and makes women weep when it

blooms. At the center of the planet west is a rolling, trackless wasteland that imitates the crags and mesas of Monument Valley on earth and is a place where lightning strikes twice.

Combat on the planet west has more etiquette than the altar, bedroom, and courtroom combined. The six-gun is Excalibur, the Winchester is a lightning bolt, and the Gatling gun is the Strategic Defense Initiative. The good routinely survive arrow wounds. The only doctor in a hundred miles can always extract a bullet with forceps, proverbs, and whiskey. No one dies of stray bullets; Indians do not kill children; killing an Indian is not murder. Then again, murder is not as heinous as rustling and a trivial third to horse thieving. Backshooting is a mark of Cain; Abel's folly was to take off his guns.

There is a 25-mile-per-hour railroad that is perpetually coming, from some place east toward some place west, always one track, with trestles built over the deepest available gulches. The homesteaders fence off the range like mad spiders, yet never seem to grow anything but complaints and children. The cattlemen, on the other hand, are a bawdy, sentimental bunch who dwell on ranches called spreads because they are bigger than the Crimea. Their cattle, outfitted with horns wider than Beelzebub's, often spook and stampede everything flat.

Other wildlife includes burros, buzzards, coyotes, songbirds, mountain lions, grizzly bears, and rattlesnakes; dogs are rare, cats and buffalo invisible. The greatest animal is the horse, a faithful, tireless, mortal creature, careless of gun-

Storm clouds roll over the wide, flat landscape of the west, where lightning strikes twice.

In the nighttime landscape of the west, the moon is usually full and always fixin' to rise.

fire and keen on galloping down Main Street. Also, the horse is many-colored, though black and white are prized, and a paint or speckled horse confers intelligence upon the rider. No man eats horsemeat, and any cowboy would sooner quit beauty than a good pony.

The towns on the planet west bear compelling names like Warlock, Deadlock, Shinbone, Bottleneck, Deadwood, Tombstone, Dodge City, Chuckaluck, Laredo, Tucson, Silver City, Helldorado, San Miguel, Eldorado. Big towns are mentioned but not visited. San Francisco is known as the city of dreams and fancy women and New Orleans the city of memories and fancy women. Los Angeles does not exist, nor do Dallas, Houston, Denver, Las Vegas, or Mexico City.

The towns themselves are built out of unpainted planks, sandstone, and copper sod and provide a predictable collection of shopwindow targets that are tucked between saloons as bright and roomy as the Metropolitan Opera. The approved saloon pastime is poker; the disapproved pastime is cheating at poker. The hotel has two floors, a useful balcony, wallpaper, and a tart in every bed. The jailhouse is a fortress but must have a back window that can be wrenched out. The church is either adobe, run by berobed missionaries and peopled by peasants, or, if Protestant, half-built and the pride of the territory. And the gallows, constructed noisily overnight, draw a bigger crowd than would any touring president except Grant. The penitentiary at the never-located Yuma makes men weep.

The planet west is certainly no place to visit, yet it is a cowboy's homey fantasy. In truth, that is the secret to the western movie. Yes, it is a cattle drive of myths, and yes it is a boyish parade, but yes too, the western, being timeless, is out there in the space of the mind's eye as a utopian vision, what the audience wants both America to become—land of the free, home of the brave—and the world too: California or Bust.

The cowboy truly means to tame his west, clean it up, and make it safe for both Sunday-goin'-to-meetin' homesteadin' folk and home-on-the-open-range cowpokes. He truly means to create the best of all possible worlds, where a man can trap, hunt, fish, ramble, scuffle, gamble, drink, whore, laugh, sleep like a bear cub under Heaven, and if he must, marry too.

That is why, when folk ask nowadays, whatever happened to the western movie, how come Hollywood does not make them anymore the way they used to, the answer is, they do. Utopia is where you look for it. The phenomenon of *Star Trek* and its camp followers has more to do with *Stagecoach, Red River, The Searchers,* and *Shane* than it does with UFOs and NASA. And would one have it any other way, that someday in the twenty-first century, the two most fanatically utopian-minded nations on earth will finally combine their mythic and cosmic ambitions for freedom and vainglory and launch a noisy stagecoach to the stars, the Russian and the American Ringo Kid, Thomas Dunson and Ethan Edwards on their way west.

Westward Ho!

John R. Hamilton's photographs present the timelessly dusty images of the western. These are not pictures out of any particular movie; these are representations of the power of the western corpus. To consider these one hundred and thirty is to relive every western you have ever seen once or ten times. Pictures like these are the joy of the myth, needing only a plot, a growl, and popcorn to awaken the cowboy movie the audience wants to live inside of forever.

Hamilton's thirty years of western work began with John Ford's masterwork, *The Searchers* (1956), and reaches to date to *Silverado* (1985), Lawrence Kasdan's measured tribute to Ford. Not only are these photographs a collective memory of the make-believe west, they also provide a ready window on the martial energy necessary to assemble all those very expensive people, horses, and props to make everything happy-ever-after one more time under a sunset. What makes the westerns fun is that the moviemakers had fun at them, and this is equally true for Hamilton's adventure.

What is not obvious in the collection, however, and yet what empowers it, is the roadmap of these movie locations. From Monument Valley and Moab, Utah to Old Tucson, Arizona; Durango, Mexico; Boulder, Colorado; Death Valley and Las Vegas, Nevada; Bracketville, Texas; Eugene, Oregon; Lone Pine and Indio, California; Santa Fe, Gallup, and Albuquerque, New Mexico, and even Elat, Israel, Jack Hamilton has packed a reflex camera and a child's-eye view. His reminiscence could serve for those of all the western play actors everywhere, "When I was young, I played cowboys and Indians and it excited me. I used to think on the sets, hey, they're paying me for this. I loved it."

JOHN CALVIN BATCHELOR

The camera moves along these dolly tracks, following the action during the course of a scene. The tracks must be level to prevent the camera from jogging. OPPOSITE: the wheels of a stagecoach churn up dust as the stage speeds on its journey.

${R}$odriguez translates for the captured Apache girl in *Rio Conchos:* "The Apache will water the land with the blood of the white eyes who have stolen it."

The Indian chief surveys his land with a rugged, enigmatic stare.

These skeleton dolls, whose wooden bodies clatter menacingly against each other, were used in a fiesta scene in *The Legend of the Lone Ranger,* 1980.

John Wayne, *center,* and comrades round up stray horses at a watering hole in *The Sons of Katie Elder,* 1965.

LEFT: all pales beside the horse, that faithful and tireless creature without which the cowboy could not exist. ABOVE: it is also the mount of the Indian. Here, ritualistic painting has prepared the horse for an ambush ride.

TOP LEFT: teepees are an essential part of that land where all westerns take place. BOTTOM LEFT: a makeup kit filled with various jars and cans of makeup, brushes, and sponges. The cases are strong enough for the makeup artist to sit on. ABOVE: the movies left their own ghost towns. OPPOSITE: even on a sunny day, floodlights may be needed for filming.

Thunder in the Dust

In the best of the westerns, the Indian is the nightmare you wake from.

This warrior exhibits the epic fierceness which the western bestowed on his kind.

Sure is rough looking country," remarks Wyatt Earp, looking out at Monument Valley in John Ford's *My Darling Clementine*. "Ain't no cow country. Mighty different where I come from. What do they call this place?"

"Just over the rise there," points the evil Pa Clanton, "big town, called Tombstone."

"Tombstone," nods Earp, "yeah, I heard of it. Well, me and my brothers might ride in there tonight and get a glass of beer."

"Yeah, enjoy yourself," says Clanton, "wide awake, wide open town, Tombstone, get anything you want there."

Ford's Point in Monument Valley was named after director John Ford, who filmed some of his greatest westerns at this breathtaking location. OVERLEAF: the camera crew captures an action sequence in Ford's *Cheyenne Autumn*, 1964.

Filmmakers have traveled even to Israel to find locations for the planet west. OPPOSITE: John Ford considered himself "just a hardworking, run-of-the-mill director." OVERLEAF: Ford poses in Monument Valley.

Thunder in the Dust

Lawrence Kasdan, director of *Silverado*, stands in silhouette with his cowboy hat in place. RIGHT: Gordon Douglas directs Richard Boone, *foreground*, in *Rio Conchos*, 1964.

74

Ben Johnson in *The Red Pony,* 1972.

Brigitte Bardot and Jeanne Moreau in *Viva Maria,* 1965.

Henry Fonda in *The Red Pony,* 1972.

Thunder in the Dust

Robert Mitchum in *El Dorado*, 1967.

Frank Sinatra in *Sergeants 3*, 1962.

Paul Newman in *Hombre*, 1967.

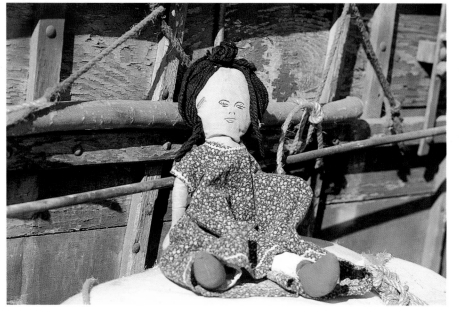

In westerns, women are usually heavily clothed. Wrapped in shawls, their hair hidden in bonnets, they must be ready to respond to the threats that the world of cowboys and Indians throws their way.

The stagecoach occupies a crucial place in the lore of the western, carrying its crew of motley passengers across the country—always a prime target for ambush.

Hollywood looked to all sorts to play Indians.
ABOVE: Gilbert Roland fords a river.

They certainly are a fine looking bunch of soldier boys back there," says the corrupt banker Gatewood in *Stagecoach*. "Always gives me a feeling of pride in our country to see the splendid men that serve in our army."

Before the western cavalry rides to the rescue, they must rehearse.

There's nothin' like a good smoke and a cup of coffee," observes Johnny Logan in Nicholas Ray's *Johnny Guitar.* "You know some men got the cravin' for gold and silver. Others need lots of land or herds of cattle. And there's those that got the weakness for whiskey and for women. When you boil it all down, what does a man really need? Just a smoke and a cup of coffee."

PRECEDING PAGES
PAGE 88: the cavalry guards the stage from the perils of Indian country. PAGE 89: Cheyenne Indians on the move. The Cheyenne are among the tribes elected to be the cowboy's favorite enemy in countless westerns. PAGES 90–91: the largest gathering of oxen for a film took place during the shooting of *The Way West* in Eugene, Oregon, 1967. PAGE 92: at times, Mexicans were substituted for Indians as villain. Here, *vaqueros* chase wild horses across a stream. PAGE 93: hundreds of horses were rounded up from all over Mexico for the filming of *The Sons of Katie Elder.* OPPOSITE: the spectacular dawn roundup scene from *The Sons of Katie Elder* lasted less than a minute, but Mexican cowboys were paid $10 a head for the 500 horses used. Durango, Mexico, 1965.

There's nothin' like a good smoke and a cup of coffee," observes Johnny Logan in Nicholas Ray's *Johnny Guitar*. "You know some men got the cravin' for gold and silver. Others need lots of land or herds of cattle. And there's those that got the weakness for whiskey and for women. When you boil it all down, what does a man really need? Just a smoke and a cup of coffee."

Preceding pages
Page 88: the cavalry guards the stage from the perils of Indian country. Page 89: Cheyenne Indians on the move. The Cheyenne are among the tribes elected to be the cowboy's favorite enemy in countless westerns. Pages 90–91: the largest gathering of oxen for a film took place during the shooting of *The Way West* in Eugene, Oregon, 1967. Page 92: at times, Mexicans were substituted for Indians as villain. Here, *vaqueros* chase wild horses across a stream. Page 93: hundreds of horses were rounded up from all over Mexico for the filming of *The Sons of Katie Elder*. Opposite: the spectacular dawn roundup scene from *The Sons of Katie Elder* lasted less than a minute, but Mexican cowboys were paid $10 a head for the 500 horses used. Durango, Mexico, 1965.

Why don't we take a walk," proposes Kathleen Lloyd to Jack Nicholson in Arthur Penn's *Missouri Breaks,* "and we'll talk about the wild west and how to get out of it."

PRECEDING PAGES
PAGE 96: the greatest animal is the horse. PAGE 97: the cattle of the west, outfitted with horns wider than Beelzebub's, often spook and stampede everything flat. PAGE 98: stalwart oxen at times are employed to pull a pioneer wagon across a river. PAGE 99: horses, however, often lead the way. RIGHT: a mother and child in *Silverado,* 1985. FAR RIGHT: Slim Pickens and Van Heflin in the cutaway stage on a flatbed truck during *Stagecoach,* 1966.

Rosanna Arquette on the set of *Silverado*, 1985.
OVERLEAF: a stage tears across Monument Valley.

William Holden in *The Horse Soldiers,* 1959. RIGHT: in the western, an Indian raiding party tearing down from the hills inspires epic levels of terror.

104

Preceding pages

Page 106: "Bugler sound charge . . . and follow me!"
Page 107: the cowboy is the Declaration of Independence, the Constitution, and the Bill of Rights all at once, with the grandly fun amendment that he exists in motion amount. Pages 108 and 109: the battles and chases are the heart of the western. Above: stern Indian faces. Right: what could be more terrible? Indians with torches plan to set fire to tumbleweed.

The attack increases in speed and intensity until it
is almost unbearable.

ABOVE, LEFT, AND OVERLEAF: stunt riding adds to the excitement, as riders fall dangerously close to campfires or are dragged through the dust.

"Faster, you fool," screams Gatewood in *Stagecoach*. "They're gaining!" Curly leans down and hands him his six-gun. "Shut up and use this."

A stunt driver triggers a fire in the coach by hitting a trip with his foot. ABOVE: the water churning around the wagon hitch accents the perils of a river crossing.

The cowboy is frontier justice incarnate, come to earth to make thunder in the dust. OVERLEAF: in his fight for freedom, the cowboy takes things into his own hands. PAGE 123, TOP: Alex Cord plays Ringo in *Stagecoach,* the role of passionate, outsized cowboy that made John Wayne a star. BOTTOM: Steve McQueen tracks down his parents' killers in *Nevada Smith,* 1966.

ABOVE: Van Heflin in *Stagecoach,* 1966. LEFT: Kirk Douglas in *The Way West,* 1967. OPPOSITE: John Wayne in *El Dorado,* 1967.

You went out there to talk," asks a pioneer woman of John Henry (John Wayne) in Andrew V. McLaglen's *Undefeated,* "why'd you have to shoot the man?"

John Henry answers, "Conversation kind of dried up, ma'am."

OPPOSITE: Kevin Kline enters a saloon, an essential landmark in the cowboy's landscape, in *Silverado,* 1985. ABOVE: Jason Robards in *The Legend of the Lone Ranger,* 1980. TOP RIGHT: Brigitte Bardot in *Viva Maria,* 1965. RIGHT: Richard Widmark in *Cheyenne Autumn,* 1964.

TOP LEFT: Jack Warden in *Billy Two Hat*, 1972. BOTTOM LEFT: a cowboy extra takes five. BELOW: Dean Martin in *Sergeants 3*, 1962. OPPOSITE: the special effects crew uses sprinklers to create this rainy night scene on a back lot. OVERLEAF: Alex Cord races in pursuit of the runaway stage in the aftermath of an Indian attack in *Stagecoach*. PAGE 131: John Wayne takes a break during the filming of *The Sons of Katie Elder*.

I thought Indians were supposed to be hard to sneak up on," says Josey Wales in *The Outlaw Josey Wales.*

The old Indian returns, "I'm an Indian all right, but here in the Indian Territory they call us the civilized nation. They call us civilized because we're easy to sneak up on."

Indians ford a river on their way home. OVERLEAF: at the center of the west is a rolling, trackless wasteland. PAGES 136 AND 137: there is one blazing sun but no finite horizon, so one assumes the west is bordered by fire.

As for you, Horace Greeley," proclaims newspaper editor Dutton Peabody to thin air in John Ford's *The Man Who Shot Liberty Valance,* "go West, old man, and grow young with the country!"

A solitary cowboy, alone in the wilderness, his accordion a clue to this being only a movie.

As many as 250 people on the set must be fed, and their contracts call for hot meals; horses pull prairie schooners down a highway to the next location.

ABOVE LEFT: a young extra takes a break on the set of *The Way West.* ABOVE: the ranch house cook prepares a meal in *The Legend of the Lone Ranger,* 1980. OPPOSITE: a horse wrangler on the set of *Cheyenne Autumn.* Each wrangler is responsible for five horses.

Thunder in the Dust

When winter hits in the western, it does so on an epic scale. OPPOSITE: Indians trek through a fresh Colorado snowfall in subzero temperatures.

Thunder in the Dust

OPPOSITE: soldiers set out to shoot a scene, leaving the prop trucks on the highway. ABOVE: faithful, tireless horses bear up under the cold. OVERLEAF: a saloon at magic hour—movie talk for twilight— shines like a beacon to cowboys still in the saddle. PAGE 149: the crew of *Silverado* seems to be scaling its own frontier. PAGES 150–151: the planet west is a cattle drive of myths and a boyish parade.

Thunder in the Dust

PRECEDING PAGES: the watch at dusk; the ride into the sunset. In the western it's clear that any resolution is only temporary. LEFT AND ABOVE: it is not the western United States that is on the screen; it is the *west* — a timeless never-never land of great expectations and grand illusions. OVERLEAF: the cowboy truly means to tame the west; he truly means to create the best of all possible worlds.

155

Well, why don't you say it, we're beat and you know it!" exclaims Martin Pawley in John Ford's *The Searchers,* about their five year search to find the Indian-kidnapped Emily Edwards.

"Nope, we're turnin' back don't mean nothing," responds Ethan Edwards, "not in the long run. If she's alive, she's safe for awhile. They'll keep her to raise as one of their own, till she's of the age to, uh—"

"Do you think there's a chance we still might find her?"

"Indian'll chase a thing till he thinks he's chased it enough, and quits," declaims Ethan Edwards. "Same way when he runs. Seems like he never learns there's such a thing as a critter that just keeps comin' on. We'll find 'em in the end, I promise you, we'll find 'em, just as sure as the turnin' of the earth."

Design
———
J. C. Suarès
Jeff Batzli

Composed in Baskerville by Arkotype Inc., New
York, New York
Printed and bound by Dai Nippon Printing Co.,
Ltd., Tokyo, Japan